Daniela Aparecida Estevan
Ana Odete Santos Vieira
Ricardo Tadeu de Faria

Bromeliaceae from the north-eastern region of the state of Paraná, Brazil

Daniela Aparecida Estevan
Ana Odete Santos Vieira
Ricardo Tadeu de Faria

Bromeliaceae from the north-eastern region of the state of Paraná, Brazil

Bromeliads

ScienciaScripts

Imprint

Cover image: www.ingimage.com

This book is a translation from the original published under ISBN 978-3-330-76070-7.

Publisher:
Sciencia Scripts
is a trademark of
Dodo Books Indian Ocean Ltd. and OmniScriptum S.R.L publishing group

120 High Road, East Finchley, London, N2 9ED, United Kingdom
Str. Armeneasca 28/1, office 1, Chisinau MD-2012, Republic of Moldova, Europe
Printed at: see last page
ISBN: 978-620-8-34207-4

SUMMARY

A study was carried out on the family Bromeliaceae A.Juss. (order Poales) in the north-eastern region of the state of Paraná (Brazil) (23°-24.5° S and 49.5°-51.5° W), which is mainly covered by Semideciduous Stationary Forest. The aim was to find out more about the richness of the family, indicate morphological characteristics that are important for recognising the species, using identification keys and descriptions, as well as updating geographical distributions. The work was carried out through collections in 35 municipalities to analyse living plants and expand herborised material deposited in herbaria, as well as consulting the collections of herbaria in Paraná. This family is represented in the region by 36 species, belonging to the genera *Tillandsia* (11 species), *Dyckia* (nine), *Billbergia* (five), *Aechmea* and *Vriesea* (three), *Acanthostachys, Ananas, Bromelia, Pitcairnia* and *Wittrockia* (one species each). The species are distinguished by the type of habit (epiphytic or rupicolous), leaf characteristics (entire margin or spinescent, forming a rosette or not), inflorescence (simple or compound, pedunculate or sessile), sepals (free or fused, symmetrical or asymmetrical), presence of petal appendages, presence of infructescence, type of fruit (berry or capsule) and presence of comose seeds. A key for genus identification was proposed, as well as descriptions and illustrations of the species. Of the total, 16 species are not protected in Conservation Units in Paraná, three species of *Dyckia* are mentioned as occurring only in the state of Paraná, and two of these are recorded in just one locality.

Keywords: bromeliads, epiphytes, taxonomy, Atlantic rainforest, southern Brazil.

* PhD Thesis in Agronomy - State University of Londrina, Londrina, 2010.

CONTENTS

CHAPTER 1

BROMELIACEAE FAMILY

Bromeliaceae A.Juss. is a family of monocotyledonous angiosperms of significant beauty and ecological importance in ecosystems. It is currently included among the 16 families of the order Poales (APG III, 2009). The family consists of 58 genera and 3352 species (LUTHER, 2012) distributed almost exclusively on the American continent, except for *Pitcairnia feliciana* (A.Chev.) Harms & Mildbr., a species that occurs in Africa (ALVES et al., 2015, BENZING, 2000; WANDERLEY et al. 2009).

The bromeliads, known as *karatas* by the natives of the Antilles, were named at the end of the 17th century by the French explorer and botanist Charles Plumier, who called them bromeliads in honour of the Swedish botanist Olaf Bromei (CARVALHO, 2003). Smith and Downs (1974) characterise three important centres of genetic diversity and dispersal of bromeliad species: the Andean region with extensions towards Mexico and the Antilles, the east coast of Brazil, represented by the Atlantic Forest biome and the Guiana Shield.

The monophyly of the family is supported by molecular characteristics, possibly including the basic chromosome number of 25, and morphological characteristics such as the presence of septal nectaries, which must be a plesiomorphy within the group (JUDD et al., 2009).

The family has traditionally been divided into three subfamilies: Pitcaimioideae (winged seeds), Tillandsioideae (comous seeds) and Bromelioideae (fleshy fruits) (SMITH & DOWNS, 1974). Bromelioideae would have a completely infertile ovary (except for *Acanthostachys* with a partially succulent ovary) and indehiscent fruits with seeds without appendages, unlike the subfamilies Pitcaimioideae and Tillandsioideae with a partially or completely succulent ovary and capsular fruits and seeds with appendages (comosas). The Pitcaimioideae subfamily, with terrestrial plant species with generally aculeate leaves and entire seed appendages, differs from the

Tillandsioideae subfamily whose plants are generally epiphytes with leaves that always have entire margins and have feathery seed appendages (REITZ, 1983).

However, more recent classifications acknowledge the parallelism of Pitcaimioideae and recognise eight subfamilies: Tillandsioideae, Bromelioideae (monophyletic), Hechtioideae, Navioideae, Pitcaimioideae, Puyoideae, Brocchinioideae and Lindmanioideae (GIVNISH et al. 2011). Natural hybridisation and the development of varieties for economic purposes, mainly ornamental, make it even more difficult to delimit genera, list taxa and conserve the family, requiring more accurate studies of the phylogeny of bromeliads (GIVNISH et al., 2011).

Many bromeliad species have high ornamental potential, mainly due to the great variety in the shape, colour and number of their leaves, which are usually arranged in rosettes, and their inflorescences with colourful bracts. In addition to their use in floriculture and landscaping, they have significant economic importance as food (Ananas), pharmacological use (Bromelia, *Tillandsia)* or fibre production for commercial purposes (Ananas, *Bromelia*) (REITZ, 1983).

With the growth and development of urban and agricultural areas, Brazilian vegetation has been suffering intense reduction and degradation. In addition to losing their natural habitats, bromeliads are extracted from their natural habitat to be sold as ornamental plants, and have historically been removed and destroyed in large quantities because they are considered harmful, acting as breeding grounds for insect larvae that cause disease. These factors have caused and still cause a decrease in the population of certain species, consequently aggravating their danger of extinction, with 202 species listed in the Red Book of Brazilian Flora (MARTINELLI & MORAES, 2013).

1.1. General ecological characteristics

A recent review on pollination in neotropical Poales pointed to birds as the main pollinators in the family, but other syndromes and mixed pollination systems have been reported (WOLOWSKI & FREITAS, 2015). In Paraná, a study of eight species of bromeliads in a dense ombrophilous forest (KAEHLER et al., 2005) identified 12 species of pollinators, eight of which were hummingbirds, three bats and one bee. The size of the corolla and the time of anthesis, as well as the presence of odour and nectar were shown to determine the group that acts as pollinators, with the formation of distinct guilds between groups of bromeliad species.

A review of data on the reproductive system showed a preponderance of self-compatible species (WOLOWSKI & FREITAS, 2015), but the process of self-fertilisation seems to be rare in bromeliads, as the flowers are usually protandric (BENZING, 2000; REITZ, 1983).

Bromeliads have zoochoric or anemochoric dispersal, with species with fleshy fruits adapted to endozoochoric dispersal, preferably carried out by frugivorous birds, while species with capsule-type fruits have seeds dispersed by the wind (BENZING, 2000; REITZ, 1983).

Vegetative reproduction is considered an advantageous strategy in different situations, especially when occupying new environments, and often favours the formation of large colonies. This propagation can occur by axial shoots from rosette leaves or by rhizomes or stolons in terrestrial species (REITZ, 1983).

Many bromeliad populations survive seasonal drought and exposure to the sun when on rocks or epiphytes, and have adaptations for these environments. In addition to their ability to absorb water and nutrients, trichomes help to reflect light and protect against excessive transpiration (BENZING, 2000; REITZ, 1983). The epidermis and cuticle slow down water loss and drastically reduce the intensity of light reaching the inner cells and, consequently, the leaf's chlorophyll. Many species of bromeliad have the CAM metabolism (Crassulacean Acid Metabolism) which promotes water saving (BENZING, 2000).

1.2. The Bromeliaceae family in Brazil

In Brazil, the family is represented by around 44 genera and 1343 species, 1174 of which are endemic (FORZZA et al., 2015), data from a series of monographs of genera and local floras (ALVES, et al., 2015). Bromeliads occur in all biomes and different forest and grassland formations of the Atlantic Forest, restingas, campos rupestres, campos de altitude, caatinga and in some regions of the Amazon and Pantanal (TARDIVO & CERVI, 1997a). The Atlantic Forest biome has the greatest diversity and cases of endemism, with 31 genera and 803 species, ten of which are endemic to this biome (MARTINELLI et al., 2008).

1.3. Family studies in Paraná and neighbouring states

In the state of Paraná, 20 genera, 105 native species and two exotic species are cited for the Bromeliaceae family (KAEHLER et al. 2014). There are no comprehensive studies related to the family, only taxonomic treatments for genera (TARDIVO & CERVI, 1997a, 1997b; KOWALSKI & TARDIVO, 2015), floristic studies of the family in specific localities (TARDIVO & CERVI, 2001), or on vascular epiphytes (BONNET et al., 2010a, 2010b; BORGO et al., 2002; BORGO & SILVA, 2003; CERVI & BORGO, 2007; DETTKE et al., 2008; GAIOTTO & ACRA, 2005; HEFLER & FAUSTIONI, 2004; KERSTEN & SILVA, 2001, 2002; KERSTEN & KUNIYOSH, 2009).

Important taxonomic studies have been carried out in the neighbouring states of São Paulo (WANDERLEY & MARTINS, 2007) and Santa Catarina (REITZ, 1983). For the state of Santa Catarina, 105 species belonging to 16 genera were found (REITZ, 1983). All the genera and 73 species from this total of Santa Catarina species were also cited for the state of Paraná in the same study. For the state of São Paulo, as a result of the "Flora Phanerogamica" project, 160 species in 18 genera were recorded, with six species not described because only type or photographic records were found.

Martinelli et al. (2008) found a deficiency in the number of specimens preserved in herbaria, with the states of Rio de Janeiro, São Paulo and Espírito Santo having the highest number of specimens of the family deposited in herbaria. According to the same author, policies to encourage herbaria to expand their collections are necessary, as the lack of specimens jeopardises progress in knowledge of the group, diversity and distribution of bromeliads (MARTINELLI et al., 2008).

1.4. Bromeliads - Importance and conservation

The greatest diversity of the Bromeliaceae family occurs in the Atlantic Forest biome, which covered a large part of the state of Paraná at the beginning of the century (83.4 per cent), but data from 1990 estimates that only 5.2 per cent of forested area remains in the state (LOUREIRO, 2004).

The mere existence of fragments is not enough to guarantee the preservation and conservation of diversity, as the composition and abundance of epiphytic bromeliads vary between the successional stages of a forest, as they depend on microclimatic conditions due to their strategy for obtaining nutrients, as well as the length of time the substrate is available for colonisation. Tank-forming species in particular need well-preserved fragments or those in more advanced stages of succession (BONNET & QUEIROZ, 2006).For bromeliad species, in addition to the fragmentation of forests and the destruction of natural environments, another aggravating factor is the intense extraction of individuals from naturally occurring sites to be used as ornamentals. The official lists of species at risk of extinction indicate that 40 per cent of bromeliad species in the Atlantic Forest are in some category of threat of extinction, and 338 taxa are cited for the whole of Brazil. However, according to Martinelli et al. (2008), it is likely that this number is underestimated due to the lack of knowledge of the actual conservation status of populations in natural environments and the small number of specimens deposited in herbaria, which jeopardises the assessment of the geographical distribution of taxa.

The extinction or decline of bromeliad populations alters important ecological processes in ecosystems, given the range of interactions between bromeliads and representatives of fauna and flora. The water reservoir (pond) of bromeliads serves as a habitat for both fauna (tree frogs, lizards, small snakes, spiders, scorpions, dragonflies, grasshoppers, beetles, insect larvae...) and insects, natural watering holes for mammals and birds and others) and flora (cohabitation with orchids, arachnids, mosses, gesneriaceae, peperomias, ferns, and occasionally *Clusia* or *Ficus,* and *Erythroxylon* in sandbanks), as well as algae and protozoa (BENZING, 2000; REITZ, 1983; SMITH & DOWNS, 1974). The dense populations of bromeliads in the forest canopy can also have a significant influence on mineral and hydrological cycling processes (BENZING, 2000; OLIVEIRA, 2004).

CHAPTER 2

MATERIAL AND METHODS

The study area comprises the north-eastern region of the state of Paraná, located in southern Brazil, between parallels 23° - 24.5° S and 49.5° - 51.5° W, crossed by the Tropic of Capricorn (Fig. 1). This region is located on the Second and Third Plateaus of Paraná.

The geological and pedological aspects of the region are quite heterogeneous, with tabular reliefs, "cuestas" and more dissected structural platforms formed by older Palaeozoic sediments predominating on the Second Plateau, and basaltic flows on the Third Plateau (MAACK, 1968; STIPP, 2002). The main hydrographic basins are the Rio das Cinzas and the Rio Tibagi. The climates are Cfa, Cfb and Cw, corresponding to almost all the climatic types found for the state of Paraná.

The region's vegetation is made up of different phytogeographic units (Fig. 1) such as Mixed Ombrophilous Forest, Semideciduous Stationary Forest, Grassy Steppe and Wooded Savannah (IBGE, 1992; VELOSO & GÓES-FILHO, 1982).

The samples were collected in 35 municipalities in the study region (Apucarana, Arapoti, Assai, Bandeirantes, Bela Vista do Paraíso, Cambe, Congoinhas, Curiúva, Faxinai, Ibiporã, Ibaiti, Ivaí, Jacarezinho, Jaguaraíva, Jataizinho, Jundiaí do Sul, Leópolis, Londrina, Marilândia do Sul, Mauá da Serra, Nova Santa Bárbara, Ortigueira, Primeiro de Maio, Rancho Alegre, Ribeirão Claro, Santo Antônio do Paraíso, São Jerônimo da Serra, Sapopema, Sengés, Sertaneja, Sertanópolis, Tamarana, Telêmaco Borba, Tomazina and Ventania) in places where there was preserved vegetation, to analyse live plants and obtain herborised material, every fortnight from March 2006 to August 2009.

The materials collected are deposited in the FUEL herbarium. The collections of the herbaria CBT, FUEL, HUPG, MBM, UNIFIL, UPCB (acronyms according to the Catalogue of the Brazilian Herbarium Network - Botanical Society of Brazil (http://www.botanica.org.br/rbh-catalogo) and the Herbarium of the Klabin Paper Industries (HKlabin) were also analysed. For the geographical distribution of the species in the state of Paraná, the Virtual Herbarium of Flora and Fungi (http://www.splink.org.br) was consulted.

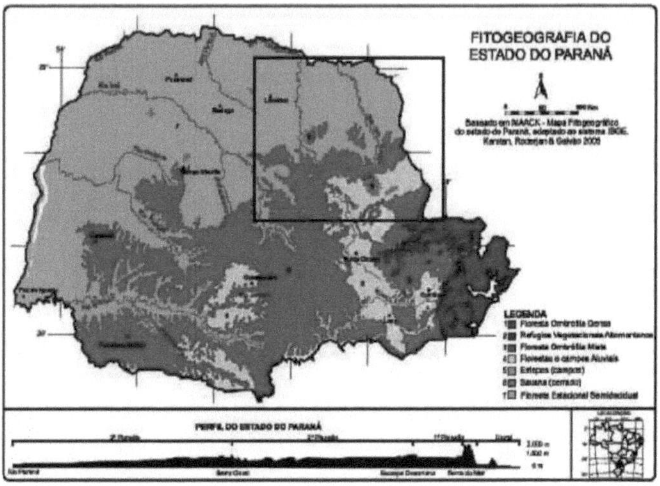

Figure 1 - Phytogeographical map of the state of Paraná. Caption: The area covered by the square represents the region studied.

The species were identified by consulting specialised bibliography, comparing the collections of the FUEL and MBM herbaria, and with the help of specialist Rosângela Capuano Tardivo.

The description of the family was based on Reitz (1983), Smith & Downs (1974) and Wanderley & Martins (2007), and of the species *Billbergia magnifica* and *B. porteana* complemented by information from Gaiotto (2005).

CHAPTER 3

BROMELIACEAE FROM THE NORTHEAST REGION OF THE STATE OF PARANÁ, BRAZIL.

The Bromeliaceae family is represented in the region studied by 36 species belonging to ten genera. The genera with the highest richness were *Tillandsia* (11 species) and *Dyckia* (nine). The list of species, their distribution in the study area (north-eastern Paraná) and their occurrence in the other municipalities of Paraná are shown in Table 1.

Bromeliaceae Juss., Gen. Pl. ed. 1.49.1789. Aug. ("Bromeliae"). nom. cons.
Type: *Bromelia* L.

Herbaceous, terrestrial, rupicolous, epiphytic or rarely shrubby. Stem usually short, rhizomatous or stoloniferous forming clumps. Leaves sheathed, simple, alternate, spiral-pinkish, polystic, forming or not forming a reservoir for water and organic debris (cistern or pond); blade margin smooth, serrated or spinescent, leaf surface coated with scales or absorbent trichomes; colour of sheath, shape and consistency of leaf blade quite varied. Scape usually conspicuous, rarely absent, partially or completely covered with bracts, usually evident and coloured. Simple (raceme, spike) or compound (paniculate, corymbiform) inflorescences or, more rarely, single flowers. Flowers sessile or pedicellate, actinomorphic or slightly zygomorphic, androgynous or sometimes functionally pistillate or staminate, trimerous, diclamydeous, heteroclamydeous; sepals free or soldered at the base, symmetrical to strongly asymmetrical; petals free or partially soldered at the base, petal appendages present or absent; stamens 6, arranged in two series, one opposite the petals and the other opposite the sepals, free or concrescent, sometimes epipetalous, anthers with longitudinal dehiscence; gynoecium tri carpellate, ovary pubescent, infertile or semiinfertile, trilocular, multilocular, axial placentation, stipe trifid. Fruit berry, capsule or compound (.-Inanas), seeds many, without appendages or appendiculate, winged or comose.

TABLE 1. SPECIES OF THE BROMELIACEAE FAMILY THAT OCCUR IN THE STUDY AREA IN THE NORTH-EASTERN REGION OF THE STATE OF PARANÁ AND THEIR RESPECTIVE OCCURRENCES IN MUNICIPALITIES IN THE STATE.

Species	Municipalities of occurrence in the state of Paraná
1. *Acanthostachys strobilacea*	Arapongas, Bela Vista do Paraíso, Cambe, Campo Mourão, Colorado, Corumbataí do Sul, Cruzeiro do Oeste, Diamante do Norte, Douradina, Fénix, Foz do Iguaçu, Ivaí, Londrina, Maringá, Poço Preto, São Jerônimo da Serra, São Pedro do Ivaí, Sengés, Telêmaco Borba, Tuneiras do Oeste, Umuarama
2. *Aechmea bromehifolia*	Capanema, Cruzeiro do Iguaçu, Guaratuba, Foz do Iguaçu, Jaguariaíva, Ortigueira, Ponta Grossa, São Jorge do Oeste Sengés, Serra Azul, Tibagi, Telêmaco Borba, Ventania
3. *Aechmea distichantha*	Adrianópolis, Apucarana, Arapoti, Araucária, Balsa Nova, Cambe, Campo Largo, Campo Mourão, Candói, Colombo, Contenda, Curitiba, Fénix, Foz do Iguaçu, Goioerê, Ibiporã, Irai do Sul, Iraquara, Iretama, Ivaiporã, Jaguariaíva, Lapa, Londrina, Maringá, Ortigueira, Palmeira, Piraquara, Ponta Grossa, Pinhais, Pinhão, Santa Terezinha de Itaipu, São Jerônimo da Serra, São Jorge do Oeste, São José dos Pinhais, São Mateus do Sul, São Miguel do Iguaçu, São Pedro do Paraná, Sapopema,

	Sertanópolis, Tamarana, Telêmaco Borba, Tibagi, Tijuca do Sul, Tomazina, Tuneiras do Oeste, Ventania
4. *Aechmea recurvata*	Antonina, Araucária, Bituruna, Campo Mourão, Carambeí, Colombo, Curitiba, General Carneiro, Guaraqueçaba, Irati, Ipiranga, Jaguariaíva, Jataizinho, Lapa, Laranjeiras do Sul, Luisiana, Mangueirinha, Mauá da Serra, Morretes, Ortigueira, Palmas, Palotina, Pinhais, Pinhão, Piraquara, Pitanga, Ponta
	Grossa, Prudentópolis, Reserva, Rio Bonito do Iguaçu, Sapopema, São Mateus do Sul, Telêmaco Borba, Três Barras do Paraná, Turvo, União da Vitória
5. *Ananas bracieaius*	Campo Mourão, Foz do Iguaçu, Matinhos, Ortigueira, Paranaguá, Telêmaco Borba, Tuneiras do Oeste, Ventania
6. *BiHbergia alfonsi-joannis*	Irati, Jundiaí do Sul, Ventania
7. *BiHbergia distachia*	Campina Grande do Sul, Cerro Azul, Guaraqueçaba, Guaratuba, Jaguariaíva, Matinhos, Morretes, Palmeira, Paranaguá, Piraquara, Quatro Barras, São José dos Pinhais, Sengés, Teixeira Soares, Tunas do Paraná
8. *BiHbergia magnifica*	Bocaiúva do Sul, Londrina, Mauá da Serra, Sapopema, Rio Branco do Sul, Tomazina, Tunas do Paraná
9. *BiHbergia nutans*	Almirante Tamandaré, Antônio Olinto, Bituruna, Campo Mourão, Cascavel, Castro, Chopinzinho,

	Cruzeiro do Iguaçu, Curitiba, Faxinai, Fénix, Foz do Iguaçu, Francisco Beltrão, General Carneiro, Guarapuava, Ipiranga, Jaguariaíva, Jataizinho, Lapa, Laranjeiras do Sul, Lobato, Londrina, Luisiana, Mandirituba, Maringá, Matelândia, Mauá da Serra, Nova Prata do Iguaçu, Ortigueira, Palmas, Palmeira, Pinhão, Ponta Grossa, Quatro Barras, Reserva, Santo Antônio do Paraiso, União da Vitória, Rio Branco do Sul, Rio Negro, São José dos Pinhais, São João do Caiuá, São Mateus do Sul, Sapopema, Tamarana, Telêmaco Borba, Tibagi, Tijucas do Sul, Tunas do Paraná, Tuneiras do Oeste, Turvo, Ventania, Xarnbrê
10. BiHbergia porteana	Jaguariaíva
11. Bromelia antiacantha	Candoí, Laranjeiras do Sul, Maringá, Paranaguá, Sapopema
12. Dyckia cabrerae	Balsa Nova, Irai do Sul, São Jerônimo da Serra
13. Dyckia crocea	Colombo, Ponta Grossa, Sengés, Tibagi
14. Dyckia dusenii	Almirante Tamandaré, Balsa Nova, Campina Grande do Sul, Imbituva, Lapa, Laranjeiras do Sul, Mauá da Serra, Ortigueira, Piraquara, Ponta Grossa, Porto Amazonas, Tibagi.
15. Dyckia leptostachya	Arapoti, Campo Mourão, Guarapuava, Guaratuba, Jaguariaíva
	Laranjeiras do Sul.
16. Dyckia lutziana	Jaguariaíva.
17. *Dyckia minaram*	Campina Grande do Sul, Jaguariaíva, Lapa, Palmeira, São Jerônimo da Serra, Tibagi.
18. Dyckia pseudococcinea	Jaguariaíva, Sengés.
19. Dyckia tuberosa	Arapoti, Balsa Nova, Campo Mourão, Castro, Jaguariaíva, Palmeira, Pirai do Sul, Ponta Grossa,

	Porto Amazonas, Sengés, Tibagi, Ventania.
20. *Dyckia walteriana*	Londrina.
21. *Pitcaimia flammea*	Campina Grande do Sul, Faxinai, Guaratuba, Jaguariaíva, Morretes, Paranaguá, Piraquara, Quatro Barras, Sengés, Tibagi.
22. *TiHandsia didisticha*	Icaraima, Jacarezinho, Porto Camargo, Telêmaco Borba.
23. *TiHandsia geminiflora*	Antonina, Campina Grande do Sul, Curitiba, Guarapuava, Guaraqueçaba, Guaratuba, Ibaiti, Jaguariaíva, Laranjeiras do Sul, Londrina, Maringá, Morretes, Matinhos, Paranaguá, Piraquara, Ponta Grossa, Pontal do Paraná, São Jerônimo da Serra, Tamarana, Telêmaco Borba, Tibagi, Tijucas do Sul.
24. *TiHandsia loliacea*	Astorga, Campo Mourão, Fénix, Jundiaí do Sul, Londrina, Rancho Alegre, Sao Jerônimo da Serra, Sertanópolis, Tumeras do Oeste.
25. *TiHandsia pohliana*	Campo Mourão, Jacarezinho, Jaguariaíva, Jundiaí do Sul, Londrina, Maringá, Nova Santa Bárbara, Paraíso do Norte, Rancho Alegre, Sengés, Tamarana, Telêmaco Borba.
26. *TiHandsia polystachia*	Londrina, Santo Antonio do Caiuá, Telêmaco Borba.
2 7. *TiHandsia recurvata*	Balsa Nova, Campo Mourão, Fénix, Guajuvira, Guarapuava, Ibiporã, Jaguariaíva, Jundiaí do Sul, Lapa, Londrina, Maringá, Palmeira, Ponta Grossa, Porto Amazonas, Sengés, Sertaneja, Telêmaco Borba, Tibagi, Tuneiras do Oeste.
28. *TiHandsia streptocarpa*	Arapoti, Assai, Balsa Nova, Campo Mourão, Leópolis, Ortigueira, Ponta Grossa, Porto Rico, São Jerônimo da Serra, São Pedro do Paraná, Sapopema,

	Tamarana, Tibagi.
29. Tillandsia stricta	Adrianópolis, Antonina, Araucária, Balsa Nova, Bela Vista do Paraíso, Campina Grande do Sul, Castro, Colombo, Curitiba, Dois
	Vizinhos, Guarapuava, Guaraqueçaba, Guaratuba, General Carneiro, Ibaiti, Ivaí, Jaguariaíva, Lapa, Laranjeiras do Sul, Londrina, Matinhos, Morretes, Ortigueira, Palmeira, Paranaguá, Pinhais, Piraquara, Pitanga, Ponta Grossa, Porto Amazonas, Quatro Barras, Rio Branco do Sul, São Jerônimo da Serra, São Jorge do Oeste, São José dos Pinhais, São Mateus do Sul, Sapopema, Sengés, Tamarana, Telêmaco Borba, Tibagi, Turvo, Ventania.
30. TiHcmdsia tenuifolia	Almirante Tamandaré, Araucária, Balsa Nova, Bela Vista do Paraíso, Bocaiuva do Sul, Campina Grande do Sul, Campo Magro, Campo Mourão, Candói, Castro, Colombo, Contenda, Coronel Domingos Soares, Curitiba, Diamante do Norte, Dois Vizinhos, Foz do Iguaçú, General Carneiro, Guaíra, Guarapuava, Guaraqueçaba, Ipiranga, Irati, Jaguariaíva, Jundiaí do Sul, Lapa, Luiziania, Lunardeli, Mandirituba, Manuel Ribas, Marechal Cândido Rondon, Marilândia do Sul, Medianeira, Ortigueira, Palmas, Palmeira, Paranaguá, Pinhão, Pirai do Sul, Piraquara, Pitanga, Ponta Grossa, Porto Amazonas, Prudentópolis, Rio Bonito do Iguaçú, Sao Jerônimo da Serra, São José da Boa Vista, São José dos Pinhais, São Mateus do Sul, Santo Antonio

	do Paraíso, Sapopema, Sertanópolis, Tamarana, Telêmaco Borba, Tibagi, Tunas do Paraná, Tuneiras do Oeste, Turvo, União da Vitoria, Vila Alta.
31. *TiHcmdsia tricholepis*	Alvorada do Sul, Bandeirantes, Campo Mourão, Comélio Procópio, Fénix, Ibiporã, Icaraíma, Ivaí, Jataizinho, Londrina, Maringá, Nova Santa Bárbara, Rancho Alegre, São Pedro do Nova Laranjeiras, Sertanópolis, Telêmaco Borba, Ventania.
32. *TiUandsia usneoides*	Araucária, Balsa Nova, Campina Grande do Sul, Castro, Colombo, Curitiba, Guaraqueçaba, Jaguariaíva, Lapa, Palmeira, Paranaguá, Piraquara, Ponta Grossa, Porto Amazonas, São Mateus do Sul, São Jerônimo da Serra, Telêmaco Borba, Tibagi, Turvo, Ventania.
33. *Vriesea flava*	Campina Grande do Sul, Doctor Ulisses, Guaratuba, Ibaiti,
	Londrina, Mauá da Serra, Piraquara, Telêmaco Borba.
34. *Vrieseafriburgensis*	Bocaiuva do Sul, Campina Grande do Sul, Colombo, Curitiba, Foz do Iguaçú, Guarapuava, Guaratuba, Iraquara, Londrina, Mandirituba, Matinhos, Mauá da Serra, Morretes, Ortigueira, Paranaguá, Piraquara, Ponta Grossa, Pontal do Paraná, São Jorge do Oeste, São José dos Pinhais, Sapopema, Sengés, Telêmaco Borba, Tibagi, Tijucas do Sul, União da Vitoria.
35. *Vriesea platynema*	Antonina, Balsa Nova, Campina Grande do Sul, Curitiba, Guaraqueçaba, Guaratuba, Iraquara, Lapa, Laranjeiras do Sul, Madirituba, Matelândia, Morretes, Paranaguá, Ponta Grossa, Quatro Barras, São Mateus do Sul, Tamarana, Tijucas do Sul,

	Turvo.
36. Wittrockia cyathiformis	Antonina, Arapoti, Balsa Nova, Campina Grande do Sul, Faxinai, Iraquara, Jaguariaíva, Lapa, Mauá da Serra, Morretes, Piraquara, Ponta Grossa, Prudentópolis, Quatro Barras, São Jerônimo da Serra, São José dos Pinhais, São Mateus do Sul, Sapopema, Tibagi, Turvo, Ventania.

IDENTIFICATION KEY FOR THE BROMELIACEAE GENERA OF THE NORTH-EASTERN REGION OF THE STATE OF PARANÁ

1. Rosette with few long (about 1 m long) pendulous leaves; two elongated, foliaceous bracts at the base of the inflorescence ....1. *Acanthostachys* (*A. strobilacea*)

1'. Rosette with many leaves, forming a pond or in the absence of a pond leaves up to 0.5 m long; absence of elongated bracts at the base of the inflorescence

2. Inflorescence with an involucre of congested bracts at the apex of the scape, or a poorly developed scape surrounded by bracts

3. Free sepals; inflorescence with conspicuous scape6 .... *Wittrockia* (*W. cyathiformis*)

3'. Sepals concrescent at base, inflorescence with inconspicuous scape2 .... .3 *Aechmea* (*A. recurvata*)

2'. Inflorescence with bracts arranged along the scape

4. Compound fruit with a crown of bracts at the apex ....3. *Ananas* (*A. bracteatus*)

4'. Simple fruit, crown of bracts absent

5. Ovary infertile; fruit berry with seeds without appendages

6. Leaves with strongly spinescent margin, the centre ones with a reddish base; petal appendages absent .... 5. *Bromelia* (*B. antiacantha*)

6'. Leaves with serrate to spinescent margin; petal appendages present

7. Inflorescence simple or compound, erect; sepals asymmetrical 2. .... *Aechmea*

7'. Inflorescence simple, pendulous; sepals symmetrical ....4. *Billbergia*

5'. Ovary succulent or semi-succulent; fruit capsule with seeds with appendages

2. Rupicolous or terrestrial plants; winged seeds

3. Leaves with a generally spinescent margin ....7. *Dyckia*

9'. Leaves with generally entire margin ....8. *Pitcairnia* (*P. flammea*)

8'. Usually epiphytic plants; feathery seeds

4. Rosette of leaves not forming a pond; petal appendages absent ....9. *Tillandsia*

10'. Rosette of leaves forming a pond; petal-like appendages present .... 10. *Vriesea*

BROMELIACEAE SPECIES FROM THE NORTH-EASTERN REGION OF THE STATE OF PARANÁ

1. *A Acanthostachys* Klotzch

This genus has only two species, *A. pitcairnioides* (Mez) Rauh & Barthlott, which only occurs in Bahia and Espírito Santo, and *A. strobilacea*, which is widely distributed (WANDERLEY & MARTINS, 2007).

1.1. *Acanthostachys strobilacea* (Schult.f.) Klotzsch in Link, Klotzsch & Otto, *Icon. Pl. Rar. 1:21, pl. 9. 1840(1841).*

Caption: Ibiporã, PR. Source: the author

Epiphyte, 0.6-1.3 m long. Short rhizomes. Leaves few, usually pendulous, not pinnate, green with whitish scales, dichotomous, linear, margin spinescent. Inflorescence spike, floral bracts orange to reddish. Flowers sessile, sepals and petals yellow. Fruit berry. Elongated, reddish-brown seeds.

Geographical distribution in Brazil: MA, MG, ES, RJ, SP and PR, in areas of Savannah and Semideciduous Stationary Forest (WANDERLEY & MARTINS, 2007, FORZZA et al., 2015).

As in the state of São Paulo, the species was only found with an epiphytic habit, although it has also been described as rupicolous (SMITH & DOWNS, 1979). This species is easy to recognise because of its few narrow-linear, pendulous leaves and its wide distribution in the study area.

Collected with flowers in September and November and fruit in June.

2. *Aechmea* Ruiz & Pav.

This genus, with 240 species (LUTHER, 2006), is the largest of the Bromelioideae subfamily, of which 184 are recorded for Brazil (FORZZA et al., 2015). Ten species of this genus are cited for the state of Paraná (KAEHLER et al., 2014), including the three found in the region studied.

2.1. *Aechmea bromeliifolia* (Rudge) Baker in Benth. & Hook. f., Gen. pl. 3:664. 1883.

Caption: Jaguaraíva, PR. Source: the author

Epiphyte or rupicolous, 07-0.9 m long. Tubular or infundibuliform rosette, densely covered with coalescing white scales. Leaves green on the upper side and pinkish on the underside, lanceolate to narrow-triangular, margin spinescent. Inflorescence simple, erect, congested, strobiliform, rachis completely covered by the flowers, densely target-lanuginous. Sepals pale green, petals yellow. Fruit berries, elliptic, crowned by a persistent perianth, sometimes densely woolly-orange.

Geographical distribution in Brazil: widely distributed, it occurs in almost all Brazilian states, in forest, restinga, savannah and grassland environments (WANDERLEY & MARTINS, 2007, FORZZA et al., 2015).

The root produces yellow dye, which gave it its popular name of gravatá-de-tingir (REITZ, 1983).

Collected with flowers in July and fruit in February, July and October.

2.2. *Aechmea distichantha* Lem. in. Jard. Fleur. 3: t.269. 1853, *nom. cons.*

Caption: Ortigueira, PR. Source: the author

Epiphyte, rupicolous or terrestrial, 0.5-1.1 m long. Tubular or infundibuliform rosette. Leaves light green to darker depending on exposure to sunlight, narrow-triangular, margin spinescent. Inflorescence compound, panicle, main raceme pink to red, white-lanceolate. Pink to red sepals and blue to lilac petals. Berries, ellipsoid, crowned by persistent sepals. Brown seeds.

Geographical distribution in Brazil: south-eastern and southern regions of Brazil, within capões, dense ombrophilous forest, restinga and rupestre fields (FORZZA et al., 2015).

The species has a wide distribution, occurring as an epiphyte both in disturbed places on roadside trees and in forest fragments, and as a rupicolous in places of greater light intensity, such as rupestrian fields and waterfall areas. According to Borgo & Silva (2003), the species occurs in forests with varying degrees of disturbance and can be called a generalist or pioneer, apparently having no survival limitations in terms of microclimatic variations (mainly light intensity and humidity). The species showed wide morphological variation in terms of the size of the plant, the shape of the rosette, the colour of the leaves, and in the inflorescence, the number of branches and flowers.

Collected with flowers from June to November and fruit in November.

2.3. *Aechmea recurvata* (Klotzsch) L.B. Sm. in. Contr. Gray Herb. 98: 5.1932.

Caption: Tamarana, PR. Source: the author

Epiphyte, 0.2-0.3 m long, rhizomatous. Rosette utriculose, subellipsoid. Leaves green to yellow-green, outermost recurved, upper leaves slightly smaller, narrowly triangular, margin spinescent. Inflorescence simple, dense, partly included in the rosette, rachis covered by the flowers. Sepals orange, red to pink and petals red to violet. Blackish fruit with persistent sepals.

Geographical distribution in Brazil: SP to RS (FORZZA et al., 2015), Mixed Ombrophilous Forest (WANDERLEY & MARTINS, 2007). In the state of São Paulo, the species' distribution is very restricted (WANDERLEY & MARTINS, 2007), which is not the case in Paraná, where it has been found in various localities and ecosystems. The species is easily recognisable by the utriculose rosette of the adult individuals and the inflorescence immersed in the leaf rosette. Young individuals, on the other hand, have narrower sheaths and poorly developed rosettes, which are not yet utriculose in shape, and can be confused with *Billbergia nutans*.

Collected with flowers in December and fruit in August and December.

3. *Ananas* Mill.

The genus has seven species that occur in Brazil (FORZZA et al., 2015), two of which are cited for the state of Paraná, including the only species recorded in the area studied (KAEHLER et al., 2014).

3.1. *Ananas bracteatus* (Lindl.) Schult. & Schult. f. in Roem. & Schult., Syst. Veg., 7(2): 1286.1830.

Caption: Ibiporã, PR. Source: the author

Terrestrial, 0.7-1.65 m long. Green outer leaves arcuately decurved, inner usually reddish to orange, suberect, narrowly triangular, margin spinescent. Scape and inflorescence pink, spike-strobiliform, with sterile bracts forming a crown at the apex. Pink sepals with a green base, purple petals, white at the base. Yellow, ovoid-cylindrical syncarpous fruit, formed by the central axis of the inflorescence with the ovaries flattened, crown of bracts at the apex of the compound fruit.

Geographical distribution in Brazil: Northeastern, Centre-Western, Southeastern and Southern states (FORZZA et al., 2015), Dense Ombrophilous and Stationary Semideciduous Forest, generally in open places (WANDERLEY & MARTINS, 2007).

For the Flora of São Paulo the bracts and sepals are described as reddish (WANDERLEY & MARTINS, 2007) and for the flora of Santa Catarina as pinkish-reddish (REITZ, 1983), while in the materials examined for this work they are pinkish.

Collected with flowers in April and July.

4. *Billbergia* Thunb.

The genus has 64 species, of which 49 occur in Brazil (FORZZA et al., 2015) and six are cited for the state of Paraná, including the five occurring in the study area (KAEHLER et al., 2014).

4.1. *Billbergia alfonsijoannis* Reitz in. R. Reitz, Annals Bot. Herb. Barbosa Rodrigues 4: 31, táb. 9. 1952; loc. cit. 4: 37.1952

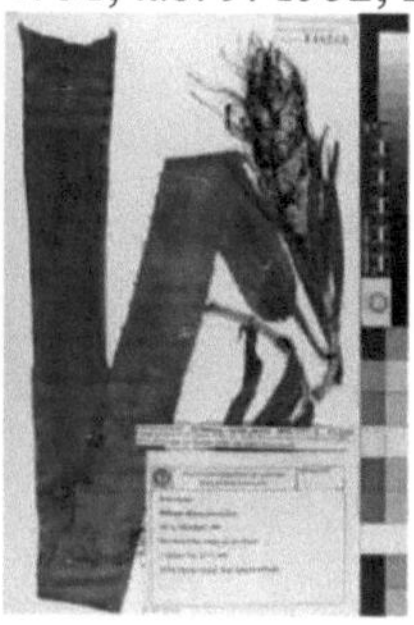

Caption: MBM herbarium exsiccata. Source: http://reflora.jbrj.gov.br

Epiphytic or terrestrial, 60 - 90 cm long. Tubular rosette. Leaves green with whitish transverse white lines, margin entire. Inflorescence densely target-lanceolate. Sepals yellow, petals yellow-green, violet towards the apex.

Geographical distribution in Brazil: MG, ES, PR and SC (FORZZA et al., 2015).

Flowering and fruiting data not available for individuals in the study area.

4.2. *Billbergia distachia* (Vell.) Mez in Mart., Eichler & Urb., Fl.bras. 3(3): 417. 1892.

Caption: MBM herbarium exsiccata. Source: http://reflora.jbrj.gov.br

Epiphyte, 60-80 cm long. Infundibuliform to tubular rosette. Leaves green to pinkish-green, narrow-triangular, serrated margin. Greenish inflorescence. Flowers ductile, sessile to short-pedicellate, sepals greenish with a blue macule at the apex, petals greenish with or without a blue macule at the apex. Fruits ovoid.

Geographical distribution in Brazil: South and Southeast of Brazil (FORZZA et al., 2015), hillside and highland dense ombrophilous forest, restinga, riparian forest and savannah (WANDERLEY & MARTINS, 2007).

Flowering and fruiting data not available for individuals in the study area.

4.3 *Billbergia magnifica* Mez in. Mez, Buli. Herb. Boiss. 11.3:133.1903

Caption: Sapopema, PR. Source: the author

Epiphyte, 40-98 cm long. Tubular rosette. Leaves green with whitish transverse white lines, erect, margin spinescent. Inflorescence target-lanuginous, sessile flowers, sepals sparsely lanuginous, petals blue towards the apex. Fruits ovoid.

Geographical distribution in Brazil: occurs only in the state of Paraná (FORZZA et al., 2015).

Flowering and fruiting data not available for individuals in the study area.

4.4. *Billbergia nutans* H. Wendl. ex Regei in. Gartenflora 18: 162. 1869.

Caption: Ventania, PR. Source: the author

Epiphytic or rupicolous, 0.35-0.6 m long. Green leaves, inner wider than outer; leathery, narrow-triangular blades, spinescent margin. Inflorescence coming from the centre of the rosette, pink to vinaceous rachis. Pink sepals with a blue apex, greenish petals with a blue tinge on the apex and margin, almost halfway down. Globose fruit, crowned at the apex by persistent sepals.

Geographical distribution in Brazil: PE, MS, SP, MG and southern Brazil (FORZZA et al., 2015), infrequent in the state of SP, found on rocky and humid slopes (WANDERLEY & MARTINS, 2007).

Collected with flowers in April to July and fruit in August.

4.5. *Billbergiaporteana* Brongn. ex Beer in. Fam. Brom.: 115. 1856

Epiphyte, 60-70 cm long. Tubular rosette. Leaves green with whitish transverse white lines, erect, margin spinescent. Inflorescence lanceolate. Sessile flowers, green or yellow-veined petals.

Geographical distribution in the area studied: there is a single record for Paraná of a collection made in Jaguaraíva by researchers Fr Raulino Reitz and Roberto Miguel Klein in 1965. However, on new excursions to the municipality, this species was not found again. If the species still exists in the wild, conservation measures should be taken

Geographical distribution in Brazil: Federal District, Paraná and the northeastern and southeastern states of Brazil (FORZZA et al., 2015), in plateau and cerrado Ombrophilous Dense Forest (WANDERLEY & MARTINS, 2007).

Flowering and fruiting data not available for individuals in the study area.

5. *Bromelia* L.

The genus includes 56 species (LUTHER, 2006), of which 46 occur in Brazil (FORZZA et al., 2015), and two are cited for Paraná, including the only species present in the north-eastern region of the state (KAEHLER et al., 2014).

5Á.Bromelia antiacantha Bertol. in. Virid. Bonon. 4. 1824; Misc. Bot. 4:6, pl. 1. 1844.

Caption: Jaguaraíva, PR. Source: the author

Terrestrial or rupicolous, 1.5-2 m long, thick stolons with a leafy apex and the rest scaly. Rosette without forming cisterns. Leaves green, the central ones with a reddish base and green towards the apex, margin spinescent. Compound inflorescence, white floral bracts. Sepals green to white, petals pink to vinaceous, usually with a smooth margin. Fruit berry, yellow, ovoid.

Geographical distribution in Brazil: BA, southeastern and southern states (FORZZA et al., 2015), in savannah, mesophytic forest, dense ombrophilous forest and restinga forest (WANDERLEY & MARTINS, 2007). This species forms large populations mainly in rocky outcrops, but is also found in the interior of forest fragments.

Collected with flowers in December and fruit in April.

6. *Dyckia* Schult. & Schult.f.

The genus consists of 141 species in Brazil (FORZZA, et al. 2015), but with serious delimitation problems, requiring taxonomic revision. The state of Paraná has the largest number of species (20) of this genus, nine of which occur in the region (KAEHLER et al., 2014).

D\..Dyc1âa cabrerae L.B.Sm. & Reitz in. Sellowia 14: 101, fig. 2, 1962

Caption: Exsiccata from the MBM herbarium. Source: http://reflora.jbrj.gov.br

Rupicule 0.3-0.5 m long. Leaves linear, slightly curved, covered in greyish scales, margin spinescent. Inflorescence simple, lax. Orange sepals and petals. Fruits ovoid capsules.

Geographical distribution in Brazil: states of Paraná and Santa Catarina (FORZZA et al., 2015).

Flowering and fruiting data not available for individuals in the study area.

6.2 *Dyckia crocea* L. B. Sm. in. Phytologia 19: 282, pl. 1, 1970.

Caption: MBM herbarium exsiccata. Source: http://reflora.jbrj.gov.br

Rupicle, 0.5-0.6 m long. Leaves green and more greyish towards the narrow-triangular sheath, margin spinescent. Simple inflorescence, canaliculate rachis, glabrous or lepidote. Flowers sessile to short-pediolate, orange petals. Fruits ovoid capsules.

Geographical distribution in Brazil: only in dry fields in Paraná (FORZZA et al., 2015, SMITH & DOWNS, 1974).

Flowering and fruiting data not available for individuals in the study area.

6.3. *Dyckia dusenii* L. B. Sm. in. Contr. Gray Herb. 98: 6, pl. 2. 1932.

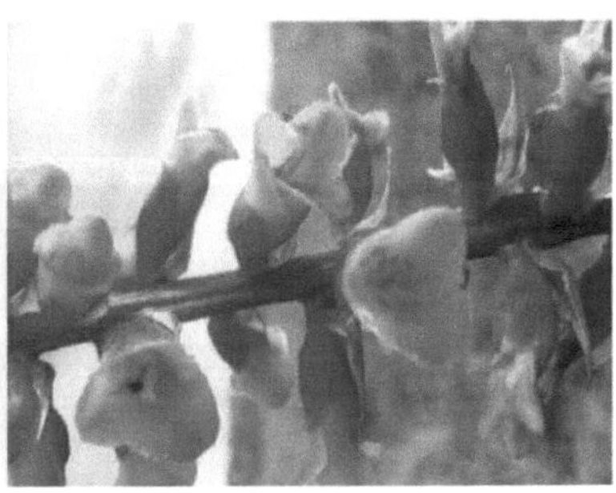

Caption: Ortigueira, PR. Source: the author

Rupicle, 0.7 metres. Leaves green and more grey towards the sheath, linear-triangular blades, spinescent margin. Inflorescence glabrous or sparsely lepidote. Red sepals, orange petals. Fruits: elliptical capsules.

Geographical distribution in Brazil: only in the states of PR and SC (FORZZA et al., 2015), at 800-950 metres above sea level (SMITH & DOWNS, 1974).

Collected with flowers and fruit in October.

5.1. *Dyckia leptostachya* Baker in. Baker, J.G., Gard. Chron., 1884(2): 198, 1884

Caption: MBM herbarium exsiccata. Source: http://reflora.jbrj.gov.br

Terrestrial, 0.4-1 m long. Outer leaves decurved and inner erect, linear-triangular, margin spinescent. Simple or branched inflorescence. Sub-sessile flowers with pedicels up to 0.4 cm long; red sepals and orange petals.

Geographical distribution in Brazil: PR, SC and RS (FORZZA et al., 2015).

Flowering and fruiting data not available for individuals in the study area.

6.5. *Dyckia lutziana* L.B. Sm. in. Arch. Bot. S. Paulo II. 1: 107, pl. 107. 1943.

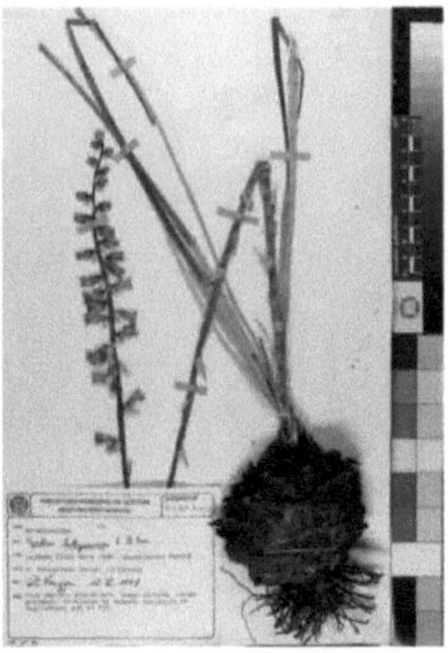

Caption: MBM herbarium exsiccata. Source: http://reflora.jbrj.gov.br

Terrestrial, 0.75 m long, pseudostem formed by the sheaths of fallen leaves. Green, linear-oblong leaves with a loosely serrated margin, target-lepidote on the upper side and almost glabrous on the underside. Simple inflorescence. Flowers sessile to short-pedicellate, yellow-orange petals.

Geographic distribution in Brazil: Smith & Downs (1974) cite a single record of the species in Brazil in the state of Paraná in an unknown locality (holotype: Foster 1144-B, Brazil, 1940 GH).

Flowering and fruiting data not available for individuals in the study area.

6.6. *Dyckia minarum* Mez in Mart., Eichler & Urb., Fl. bras. 3 (3): 483. 1894.

Caption: MBM herbarium exsiccata. Source: http://reflora.jbrj.gov.br

Rupicule, 0.8-1 m; compact stem not forming a rhizome. Leaves grey-green or slightly brown, linear-triangular, margin spinescent. Simple inflorescence. Orange sepals and petals. Fruits: elliptical capsules.

Geographical distribution in Brazil: GO, MG and SP (FORZZA et al., 2015). However, it is also found in PR.

Collected with flowers in September and fruit in December.

6.7. *Dyckiapseudococcinea* L. B. Sm. in. Arch. Bot. S. Paulo II. 1: 108, pl. 109. 1943.

Caption: MBM herbarium exsiccata. Source: http://reflora.jbrj.gov.br

Rupicule, 0.65-0.78 m long. Green, linear-triangular leaves, spinescent margin. Simple inflorescence, sessile to sub-sessile flowers, orange petals.

Geographical distribution in Brazil: according to Forzza et al. (2015) it only occurs in Rio de Janeiro.

However, it is also found in the state of Paraná.

Flowering and fruiting data not available for individuals in the study area.

6.8. *Dyckia tuberosa* (Vell.) Beer. in. Farm. Brom: 157. 1857.

Caption: Exsiccata from the MBM herbarium. Source: http://reflora.jbrj.gov.br

Rupiculate or terrestrial, 0.5 m long. Leaves greyish due to the large number of whitish scales mainly on the adaxial side, outer side arched, inner side more or less erect; triangular-lanceolate, margin spinescent. Simple inflorescence. Short-pedicellate flowers, red-orange sepals and orange petals.

Geographical distribution in Brazil: MG, SP, PR and SC (FORZZA et al., 2015), in savannah areas, inselbergs and high altitude fields (SMITH & DOWNS, 1974; WANDERLEY & MARTINS, 2007).

Collected with flowers in March and June.

6.9 *Dyckia* walteriana Leme in. Phytotaxa: 67. 2012

Caption: Assai, PR. Source: the author

Rupicolous or terrestrial, 1-2 m long, very developed rhizome covered with fragments of dried leaf sheaths. Leaves green on the adaxial side, sometimes reddish towards the apex, stiff, arranged in a dense rosette, lanceolate, margin with small spines in the upper half. Paniculate inflorescence, densely rusty-lepidote rachis. Flowers sessile to short-pediolate, sepals and petals yellow. Fruit sub-globose capsule, polished dark brown, sometimes with remains of other floral structures.

Geographical distribution in Brazil: found only in the state of Paraná (FORZZA etal, 2015).

Collected with flowers in August and September.

7. *Pitcairnia* L'Hér.

The largest genus of the Pitcaimiodeae subfamily with 350 species, 53 of which occur in Brazil (FORZZA et al., 2015), and only one in the state of Paraná (KAEHLER et al., 2014).

7.1. *Pitcairniaflammea* Lindl. in. Bot. Reg. 13: pl. 1092. 1827.

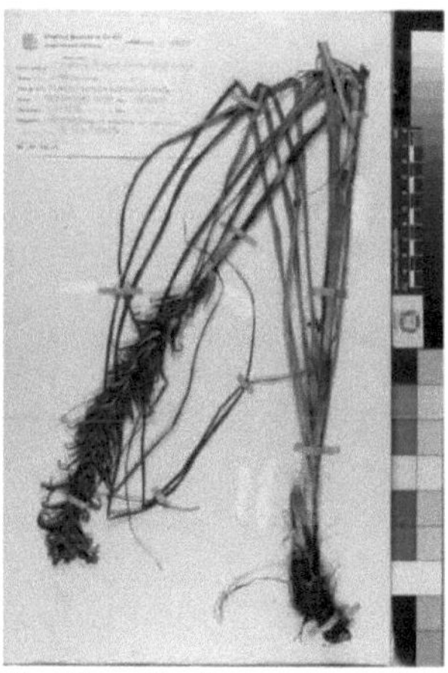

Caption: Exsiccata from the MBM herbarium. Source: http://reflora.jbrj.gov.br

Rupicle, stem usually reduced or forming elongated stolons. Green leaves with a pale midrib on the adaxial side, arched, few to many. Simple inflorescence. Sepals green to reddish-brown, petals red. Fruit capsule, ellipsoid.

Geographical distribution in Brazil: occurs from the south of Bahia to Rio Grande do Sul (FORZZA et al., 2015), often on rocks in humid areas of the Atlantic Forest (WANDERLEY & MARTINS, 2007).

Flowering and fruiting data not available for individuals in the study area.

8. *Tillandsia* L.

This is the largest genus in the family with 557 species, occurring in Tropical and Subtropical America. In Brazil the genus is represented by 87 species (FORZZA et al., 2015), and 17 are cited for the state of Paraná ((KAEHLER et al., 2014), including the 11 recorded in the study area.

8.1. *Tillandsia didisticha* (E. Morren) Baker in. Jour. Bot. London 26: 16. 1888.

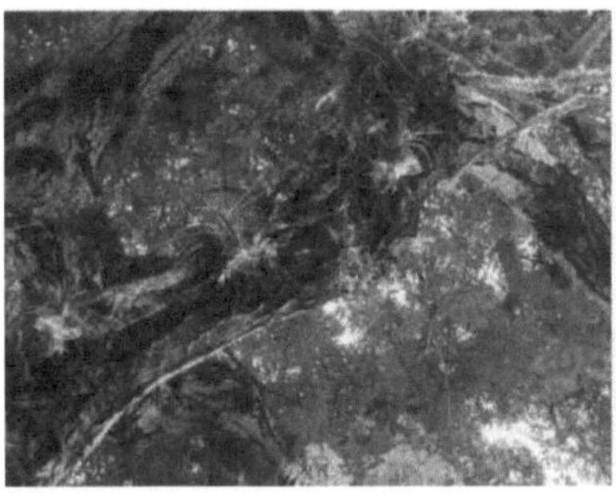

Caption: Jacarezinho, PR. Source: the author

Epiphyte, 22-27 cm long; inconspicuous stem. Leaves greyish-green, rosulate, polystic, narrow-triangular. Paniculate inflorescence. Pink sepals and white petals. Cylindrical capsule, fusiform seeds with white silky hairs.

Geographical distribution in Brazil: states of PE, GO, MS, MT and PR (FORZZA et al., 2015).

Flowering and fruiting data not available for individuals in the study area.

8.2. *Tillandsia geminiflora* Brongn. in. Voy. Monde, phan., 186. 1829.

Caption: Tamarana, PR. Source: the author

Epiphyte, 17-26 cm long, inconspicuous stem. Leaves greyish due to the dense presence of scales, turning purplish when exposed to full sun, rosulate, polystic, narrow-triangular. Compound inflorescence. Polystic flowers, pink sepals and petals. Cylindrical capsules.

Geographical distribution in Brazil: Centre-West, Northeast, Southeast and South regions of the country (FORZZA et al., 2015), extending to Paraguay and Argentina, in woodlands and savannahs (WANDERLEY & MARTINS, 2007).

Collected with flowers in May, September and October and fruit in April and December.

8.3. *Tillandsia loliacea* Mart. ex Schult. & Schult. f. in Roem. & Schult., Syst. 7(2): 1204. 1830.

Caption: Exsiccata from the MBM herbarium. Source: http://reflora.jbrj.gov.br

Epiphyte, 5-14 cm long, incospicuous stem. Leaves rosulate, polystic, erect to suberect. Simple inflorescence, ductile flowers. Brown sepals and yellow petals. Mature capsules brownish.

Geographical distribution in Brazil: Centre-West, Northeast, Southeast and South regions of the country (FORZZA et al., 2015), in caatinga, cerrado and forest regions (WANDERLEY & MARTINS, 2007). This species has a wide distribution, mainly in Semideciduous Stationary Forests.

Collected with flowers in July and August and fruit in October and December.

8.4. *Tillandsia pohliana* Mez in Mart., Eichler & Urb., Fl. bras. 3(3): 597. 1894.

Caption: Marilândia, PR. Source: the author

Epiphyte, 22-35 cm long, inconspicuous stem. Leaves greenish to greyish due to the scales, rosulate, polystic or sub-polystic, the central ones erect and the outer ones recurved, narrow-triangular. Simple inflorescence. Sepals densely lepidote and petals white. Cylindrical capsules.

Geographical distribution in Brazil: Centre-West, Northeast, Southeast and South regions of the country (FORZZA et al., 2015), occurring from Peru to Argentina, in forest and savannah (WANDERLEY & MARTINS, 2007).

Collected with flowers in September and fruit in March, April, July, August and December.

8.5. *Tillandsiapolystachia* (L.) L. in. Sp. Pl. ed. 2. 410. 1762

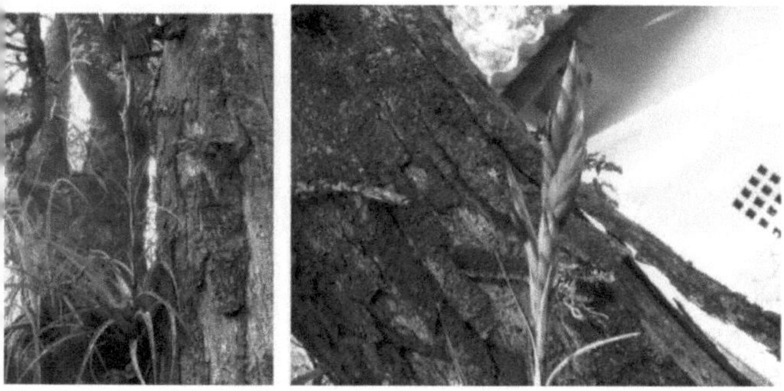

Caption: Londrina, PR. Source: the author

Epiphyte, 45-55 cm long; inconspicuous stem. Leaves greenish to greyish due to scales, rosulate, polystic, erect, triangular. Paniculate inflorescence, leathery sepals and purplish petals. Cylindrical capsules, fusiform seeds with white silky hairs.

Geographical distribution in Brazil: Northeastern, Southeastern and Southern states (FORZZA et al., 2015).

Flowering and fruiting data not available for individuals in the study area.

8.6. *Tillandsia recurvata* (L.) L. in. Sp. pl., ed. 2: 410. 1762.

Caption: Assai, PR. Source: the author

Epiphytic, 10-20 cm long, forming clumps, stem inconspicuous to conspicuous, variable in indumentum and size of stem and leaf. Leaves strongly recurved, sometimes erect, ductile, filiform to linear. Simple inflorescence. Flowers subsessile, light blue or white petals. Capsules slightly cylindrical.

Geographical distribution in Brazil: northeastern, central-western, southeastern and southern states (FORZZA et al., 2015). Widely distributed across the American continent. Found on high-voltage wires (WANDERLEY & MARTINS, 2007). Species often confused with *T. mallemontii* Glaziou ex Mez, from which it differs only by the colour of the flower.

Flowering and fruiting data not available for individuals in the study area.

8.7 *Tillandsia streptocarpa* Baker in. Jour. Bot. London 25: 241.1887.

Caption: Tomazina, PR. Source: the author

Epiphytes, 20-70 cm long, conspicuous stem. Leaves rosulate, polystic, suberect, linear-triangular, densely grey-lepidote. Simple or compound inflorescence. Dystic flowers, leathery sepals, blue to purple petals. Capsules brownish.

Geographical distribution in Brazil: PA and the north-eastern, south-eastern and southern states of the country (FORZZA et al., 2015).

Collected with flowers in April, May, July, August and November and fruit in May, July, September and December.

Flowering and fruiting data not available for individuals in the study area.

8.8. *Tillandsia stricta* Sol. in Sims, Bot. Mag. 37. 1813.

Caption: Ventania, PR. Source: the author

Epiphyte, 10-20 cm long, inconspicuous stem. Leaves pale to glaucous-green when in the shade, turning purplish when exposed to full sun, rosulate, polystic, erect, narrowly triangular. Simple inflorescence. Flowers erect or suberect, polystic, sepals pink, petals blue, turning purple, purplish. Capsules cylindrical, seeds fusiform, with white silky hairs.

Geographical distribution in Brazil: Centre-West, Northeast, Southeast and South regions of the country (FORZZA et al., 2015), wide distribution and occurrence from Venezuela to Argentina (WANDERLEY & MARTINS, 2007).

Collected with flowers in March, May, July, August and September and fruit in September.

8.9 *Tillandsia tenuifolia* L. in. Sp. pl. 286. 1753.

Caption: Sapopema, PR. Source: the author

Epiphyte, 12-30 cm long, inconspicuous to elongated stem, very variable, often branched and associated with large tangles. Leaves rosulate or arranged along the stem, polystic, erect to recurved, narrow-triangular, dense and minutely lepidote. Simple inflorescence. Polystic flowers, pink sepals and bluish petals, purplish to white. Cylindrical capsules, fusiform seeds with white silky hairs.

Geographical distribution in Brazil: Centre-West, Northeast, Southeast and South regions of the country (FORZZA et al., 2015).

Collected with flowers in August, September, October and December and fruit in March, April, September, October and December.

The species showed a great deal of morphological variation, especially in the arrangement of the leaves and the presence or absence of an obvious stem, which was also noted by Wanderley & Martins (2007).

8.10.*Tillandsia tricholepis* Baker in. Jour. Bot. London 16: 237. 1878.

Caption: Tamarana, PR. Source: the author

Epiphyte, 5-20 cm long; conspicuous stem. Leaves arranged along the stem, erect to sub-erect, densely lepidote, narrow-triangular. Simple inflorescence. Dystic flowers, leathery sepals, yellow petals. Mature capsules brownish.

Geographical distribution: Northeast, Southeast and South regions of the country

(FORZZA et al., 2015), wide distribution from Bolivia to Argentina, in forests, cerradão and campo sujo (WANDERLEY & MARTINS, 2007).

Collected with flowers in November and December and fruit in February, August, September and November.

8.11. *Tillandsia usneoides* (L.) L. in. Sp. pl., ed. 2. 411. 1762.

Caption: Jacarezinho, PR. Source: the author

Epiphyte, 3-10 cm long, forming pendulous clusters on trees up to lm or more long, stem tenuously filiform, serpentinely curved, with elongated internodes. Leaves greyish-green, ductile, filiform. Inflorescence uniflorous, inconspicuous scape. Yellow or greenish-yellow petals.

Geographical distribution in Brazil: Centre-West, Northeast, Southeast and South regions of the country (FORZZA et al., 2015), the largest distribution within the family from Florida to the south of South America, in Atlantic slope, plateau and restinga forests (WANDERLEY & MARTINS, 2007).

The population forms extensive "curtains" hanging from the trees, which makes it easy to identify the species, which is difficult to collect with flowers and fruit.

Flowering and fruiting data not available for individuals in the study area.

9. *Vriesea* Lindl.

The genus is represented in Brazil by 219 species (FORZZA et al., 2015), and 27 are cited for Paraná (KAEHLER et al., 2014), including the three that occur in the north-eastern region of the state.

9.1. *Vriesea flava* A.F. Costa, H. Luther & Wand. In. Novon 14(1): 36-39. 2004.

Caption: Ibaiti, PR. Source: the author

Epiphyte, 38-50 cm long. Infundibuliform rosette. Leaves green, ligulate-linear, apex acuminate, sparsely scaled on both sides. Inflorescence simple, distichously whorled. Yellow sepals and petals.

Geographical distribution: SP and southern Brazil (FORZZA et al., 2015), in montane rainforest (WANDERLEY & MARTINS, 2007). Species with the highest occurrence in Dense Ombrophilous Forest.

Collected with flowers in May and fruit in May and December.

9.2. *Vriesea friburgensis* Mez in Mart., Eichler & Urb. Fl. bras. 3(3): 537. 1894.

Caption: Faxinai, PR. Source: the author

Epiphyte up to 1.2 m long. Infundibuliform to utriculose rosette. Green leaves, glabrous underside and upper side with small rounded scales. Paniculate inflorescence. Dystic flowers, yellow sepals and petals. Fruits with persistent bracts and sepals.

Geographical distribution: BA, MG, RJ, SP, PR, SC and RS (Centre-West, Northeast, Southeast and South regions of the country (FORZZA et al., 2015, WANDERLEY & MARTINS, 2007).

Collected with flowers in April and September and fruit in August and December.

There are reports of the great morphological variability of the species, with regard to the number of flowers, position and length of the branches, presence of carinae and size of floral bracts and sepals, with the division into varieties that present some overlaps and disagreements in diagnostic characteristics (WANDERLEY & MARTINS, 2007), however, these characteristics were not observed in the specimens collected in the study area.

9.3. *Vrieseaplatynema* Gaudich. in. Voy. Bonite, Bot., est. 66. 1843.

Caption: Tamarana, PR. Source: the author

Epiphyte up to lm long. Infundibuliform rosette. Light green leaves with longitudinal whitish streaks, decurved from the middle upwards, glabrous on the upper side and densely covered with brownish scales on the lower side. Inflorescence raceme. Dystic flowers, green sepals, yellow petals.

Geographical distribution: SP, PR and SC (FORZZA et al., 2015), in the Atlantic rainforest (WANDERLEY & MARTINS, 2007). In the study area, it was recorded in only one locality in one municipality and few individuals were seen.

Flowering and fruiting data not available for individuals in the study area.

10. *Wittrockia* Lindm.

Exclusively Brazilian, the genus has seven species, and only two are reported for the state of Paraná (KAEHLER et al., 2014), including the only one recorded in the area studied.

10.1. *Wittrockia cyathiformis* (Vell.) Lemes, Eichler & Urb. in. Fl. Bras. 3(3): 252. 1891.

Caption: Tamarana, PR. Source: the author

Terrestrial, rupicolous or epiphytic, 42-60 cm long. Infundibuliform rosette. Leaves green, sometimes with dark green spots, margin spinescent. Inflorescence subcorymbose, pink involucral bracts and green florets. Flowers sessile, sepals greenish-orange, petals yellow. Berry fruit.

Geographical distribution: MG to SC (FORZZA et al., 2015), in dense ombrophilous forest (WANDERLEY & MARTINS, 2007).

Collected with flowers in April, May, July, October and December.

CHAPTER 4

CONCLUSIONS

The Bromeliaeceae family is represented in the state of Paraná by 105 species, of which 36 species occur in the north-eastern region of the state, a significant species richness given that the greatest diversity of bromeliads occurs in the Dense Ombrophilous Forest. The genera with the highest number of species were *Tillandsia* (11) and *Dyckia* (nine). Of the total number of species, 17 are not protected in Conservation Units in the state of Paraná, and most belong to the genus *Dyckia*, occurring in only one or a few localities.

The species B. *porteana* (collected in 1965) and D. *lutziana* (collected in 1993) have only one record in the state of Paraná, and were not found again on excursions to these localities, indicating that these species may even have become extinct. D. *pseudococcinea, D. crocea* and *T. polystachia* can also be considered rare in the state, as they are found in only three different localities (municipalities). Other species such as *D. cabrerae, D. minarum, D. leptostachya, P. flammea, T. didisticha* and *V. platynema,* despite having few collections in the area, also occur in other regions of the state.

REFERENCES

ALVES, M,; TROVÓ, M.; FORZZA, R.C.; VIANA, P. OverView of the systematics and diversity of Poales in the Neotropics with emphasis on the Brazilian flora. **Rodriguésia** 66(2): 305-328.2015.

APG III. An update of the Angiosperm Phylogeny Group classification for the orders and families of flowering plants. **Botanical Journal of the Linnean Society,** p.1-17, 2009.

BENZING, D.H. **Bromeliaceae: Profile of an Adaptive Radiation.** Cambridge: Universit Press, 2000.

BONNET, A.; QUEIROZ, M. H. Vertical stratification of epiphytic bromeliads in different successional stages of the Ombrophilous Dense Forest, Santa Catarina Island,

Santa Catarina, Brazil. **Revista Brasileira de Botanica,** v.29, n.2, p.217-228, apr.-jun. 2006.

BONNET, A.; CURCIO, G. R.; GALVAO, F.; KOZERA, C. Diversity and spatial distribution of epiphytic bromeliads of the upper Tibagi River - Paraná - Brazil. Floresta (UFPR. Impresso), v. 40, p. 71-80, 2010a.

BONNET, A.; CURCIO, G. R.; LAVORANTI, O. J.; BARDDAL, M. L.; RODERJAN, C. V. Relationships of epiphytic bromeliads with environmental factors in floodplains of the Iguaçu River, Paraná, Brazil. Floresta (UFPR. Impresso), v. 40, p. 193-208, 2010b.

BORGO, M.; SILVA, S.M.; PETEAN, M.P. Vascular epiphytes in a remnant of Semideciduous Stationary Forest, municipality of Fénix, PR, Brazil. **Acta Biológica Leopoldensia,** v.24, p. 121-130, 2002.

BORGO M.; SILVA, S.M. Vascular epiphytes in fragments of Mixed Ombrophilous Forest, Curitiba, Paraná, Brazil. **Revista Brasileira Botânica,** v.26, p.391-401, 2003.

CARVALHO, L.C. The importance and beauty of bromeliads. **Bioletim,** year III, n.3, 2003.

CERVI, A.C.; BORGO, M. Vascular epiphytes in the Iguaçu National Park, Paraná (Brazil). Preliminary survey. **Fontqueria,** Madrid, v.55, p.415-422, 2007.

DETTKE, G.A., ORFRINI, A.C.; MILANEZE-GUTIERRE, M.A. Floristic composition and distribution of vascular epiphytes in an altered remnant of Semideciduous Stationary Forest in Paraná, Brazil. **Rodriguésia,** v.59, n.4, p.859-872, 2008.

FORZZA, R.C.; COSTA, A.; SIQUEIRA FILHO, J.A.; MARTINELLI, G.; MONTEIRO, R.F.; SANTOS-SILVA, F.; SARAIVA, D. P.; PAIXÃO-SOUZA, B.; LOUZADA, R.B.; VERSIEUX, L. *Bromeliaceae* in **Lista de Espécies da Flora do Brasil.** Rio de Janeiro Botanical Garden. Available at: <http://floradobrasil.jbij.gov.br/jabot/floradobrasil/FB5920>. Accessed on: 18 June 2015.

GAIOTTO, D. F.; ACRA, L. A. Qualitative survey of epiphytes at Fazenda Gralha Azul - Fazenda Rio Grande - Paraná. **Revista Estudos de Biologia,** v.27, p.25-32, 2005.

GAIOTTO, D. F. **Taxonomic Study of the Genus *Billbergia* Thunb. (Bromeliaceae Juss.) in the State of Paraná, Brazil.** 2005. Dissertation (Master's in Botany) - Federal University of Paraná, Curitiba.

GIVINISH, T.; BARFUSS, M.; VAN E.B.; RIINA, R.; SCHULTE, K.; HORRES, R.; GONSISKA, P.; JABAILY, R.; CRAYN, D.; SMITH, J.; WINTER, K.; BROUN, G.; EVANS, T.; HOLST, B.; LUTHER, H.; TILL, W.; ZISKA, G.; BERRY, P. & SYTSMA, K. 2011. Philogeny, adaptive radiation, and historical Biogeography in Bromeliaceae: Insights from an eight-locus plastid phylogeny. **American Journal of Botany** 98: 1-24.

KHEFLER, S. M.; FAUSTIONI, P. Floristic survey of vascular epiphytes in the São Cristovão forest - Curitiba - Paraná - Brazil. **Revista Estudos de Biologia,** v.26, p.11-19, 2004.

IBGE - Brazilian Institute of Geography and Statistics Foundation. **Technical manual of Brazilian vegetation** (Série Manuais Técnicos em Geociências n.l). Rio de Janeiro: FIBGE, 1992.

JUDD, WS; CAMPBELL, C.S, KELLOGG, E.A.; STEVENS, P.F. 1999. **Plant systematics:**

a phylogenetic approach. Sunderland: Sinauer.

KAEHLER, M.; VARAS SIN, I.G.; GOLDENBERG, R. Pollination in a community of bromeliads in a high-montane Atlantic Forest in the State of Paraná, Brazil. **Revista Brasileira de Botanica,** v.28, n.2, p.219-228, apr.-jun. 2005.

KAEHLER, M., GOLDENBERG, R., EVANGELISTA, P.H.L., RIBAS, O.S., VIEIRA, A.O.S., HATSCHBAH, G.G. **Vascular plants of Paraná.** Curitiba: UFPR, 2014.

KERSTEN, R. A.; SILVA, S.M. Floristic composition and structure of the vascular epiphytic component in a coastal plain forest on Ilha do Mel, Paraná, Brazil. **Revista Brasileira de Botanica,** v.24, n.2, p.213-226, jun. 2001.

KERSTEN, R. A.; SILVA, S.M. Floristics and structure of the vascular epiphytic component in Alluvial Mixed Ombrophilous Forest of the Barigui River, Paraná, Brazil. **Revista Brasileira de Botânica,** v.25, p.259-267, 2002.

KERSTEN, R. A.; KUNIYOSH, Y.S. Forest conservation in the Upper Iguaçu Basin, Paraná - Evaluation of the vascular epiphyte community in different seral stages. **Floresta,** Curitiba, v.39, n.l, p.51-66, jan.-mar. 2009.

KOWALSKI, V.K.; TARDIVO, R.C. The *Vriesea platynema* Gaudich. group (Bromeliaceae: Tillandsioideae) in the state of Paraná, Brazil. **Rodriguésia** 66(2): 465-475. 2015

LOUREIRO, W. The current situation of Paraná's system of conservation units. In: BRAZILIAN CONGRESS OF CONSERVATION UNITS, IV, 2004. Curitiba.

Proceedings... Curitiba: O Boticário Foundation for Nature Protection and the Pro-Conservation Units Network, 2004. p. 135-148.

LUTHER, H.E. **An alphabetical list of bromeliad binomials.** 10. ed. Sarasota: The Marie Selby Botanical Gardens, 2006.

LUTHER, H. 2012. **An alphabetical list of bromeliad binomials.** 12. ed. The Bromeliad Society International. The Marie Selby Botanical Gardens, Sarasota & Bromeliad Society International, Sarasota. 44p.

MAACK, R. **Physical geography of the state of Paraná.** Curitiba: BADEP/UFPR/IBPT, 1968.

MARTINELLI, G.; VIEIRA, C.M.; GONZALES, M.; LEITMAN, P.; PIRATININGA, A.; COSTA, A.F.; FORZZA, R.C. Bromeliaceae of the Brazilian Atlantic Forest: Species list, distribution and conservation. **Rodriguésia,** v.59, n.l, p.209-258, 2008.

MARTINELLI, G. & MORAES, M. (eds.) 2013. Red Book of Brazilian **Flora**. Rio de Janeiro Botanical Garden & Andrea Jakobson Estúdio, Rio de Janeiro. HOOp.

OLIVEIRA, R.R. Importance of epiphytic bromeliads in nutrient cycling in the Atlantic Forest. **Acta Botanica Brasílica,** v.18, n.4, p.793-799, 2004.

REITZ, R. Bromeliads and the endemic malaria-bromeliad. **Illustrated Flora of Santa Catarina.** Itajaí: Barbosa Rodrigues Herbarium, 1983.

SMITH, L.B.; DOWNS, R.J. (Pitcaimioideae): Bromeliaceae. **Flora Neotropica.** New York: New York Botanical Garden, Mon.14, part.l, 1974.

SMITH, L. B.; DOWNS, R.J. Tillandsioideae (Bromeliaceae). **Flora Neotropica.** New York: New York Botanical Garden, Mon.14, part.2, 1977.

SMITH, B. L.; DOWNS, R.J. Bromelioideae (Bromeliaceae). **Flora Neotropica.** New York: New York Botanical Garden, Mon.14, part 3, 1979.

STIPP, N.A.F. The Tibagi River in the hydrogeographic context of Paraná. In: Medri, M.E.; Bianchini, E.; Shibatta, O.A.; Pimenta, J.A. (Org.). **A bacia do rio Tibagi**. Londrina, 2002. p.39-43.

TARDIVO, R. C.; CERVI, A.C. The genus *Nidularium* Lem. (Bromeliaceae) in the state of Paraná. **Acta Botanica Brasílica,** v.ll, p.237-258, 1997a.

TARDIVO, R. C. & CERVI, A.C. The genus *Canistrum* E. Morren (Bromeliaceae) in the state of Paraná. **Acta Botanica Brasílica,** v.ll, p.259-272, 1997b.

TARDIVO, R. C.; CERVI, A.C. Bromeliads of the State Park of Vila Velha, Ponta Grossa, Paraná, Brazil. **Selbyana,** v.22, p.68-74, 2001.

VELOSO, H.P.; GÓES-FILHO, L. **Fitogeografia Brasileira.** Physiognomic-ecological classification of Neotropical vegetation. Technical Bulletin RADAM-BRASIL Project, Vegetation Series, 1982.

WANDERLEY, M.G.L.; MARTINS, S.E. Bromeliaceae. **Phanerogamic Flora of the State of São Paulo.** São Paulo: Fapesp, 2007.

WANDERLEY, M.G.L., SELLARO, M. & MOREIRA, B.A. **Neotropical Bromeliaceae.** In: MILLIKEN, W., KLITGÂRD, B. & BARACAT, A. (2009 onwards), Neotropikey - Interactive key and information resources for flowering plants of the Neotropics. Available at:http ://www.kew.org/science/tropamerica/neotropikey/families/Bromeliaceae .htm). Accessed on: 18 August 2015.

WOLOWSKI, M. & FREITAS, L. An overview on pollination of the Neotropical Poales. **Rodriguésia,** v.66, n.2, p. 329-336, 2015.

MIX
Papier aus verantwortungsvollen Quellen
Paper from responsible sources
FSC® C105338

Printed by Books on Demand GmbH, Norderstedt / Germany